A Quick Crib to

VIDEO DOCUMENTARY MAKING

by Mark Patterson

BBC Television Training

First published in 1993
BBC Television Training
BBC Elstree Centre
Clarendon Road
Borehamwood
Hertfordshire

© 1993 BBC Television Training
All rights reserved
ISBN 0 948694 16 5

Throughout this book the pronoun
'she' should also be taken to refer to 'he'.

General Editor: Gordon Croton
Design and production: Shirley Greenfield
Illustrations: Nick Skelton

Printed by Able Printing Ltd
Paddock Wood
Kent
England

Contents

... put your host at ease ...

INTRODUCTION

This book is designed to help people who own or have access to a video camera or camcorder to make the best use of their equipment and to move on from basic 'home movies' to 'home documentaries'. It is not a technical text book on the use of video cameras and video editing machines but a commonsense guide to planning and executing a project using basic home video equipment.

The inspiration for the book came from recent work with the BBC's Open University when I was asked to be the consultant on a programme about using the camcorder to collect information about local history. In effect we were teaching people with limited experience of a video camera how to produce a documentary and I realised that there were many people with camcorders whose ambition went beyond *The Wedding* or *A Day at the Zoo*.

The subject we worked on was a local history project about a farmer who still milked his cows by hand. But the techniques and principles we employed are relevant to any video project. Some people may be quite happy with a wedding video that shows the bride and groom, the cutting of the cake, the best man's speech, and a few relatives pulling faces at the camera. But if you're thinking about getting the best out of your equipment the wedding can be an opportunity to capture a bit of family history for generations to come.

Wherever possible I have avoided using 'technical' words or jargon and have assumed that each person or group setting out on a video project will be fortunate enough to find one or two people who are 'good with things like cameras and tape recorders'.

I have also avoided any detailed technical descriptions of the equipment as there is such a variety of cameras and recorders on the market and each of them has switches and buttons in different places.

My approach is much simpler...your camera will have a lens on the front and somewhere to place the tape cassette. Your recorder will have a record button, a playback button and a stop button. Various cables will join all the bits together for you. What is much more important is that you get the right material on tape and assemble it in a logical and easily watchable way so that you, your family and your friends will enjoy the material you have filmed and edited.

Ruislip, Middlesex August 1993

Chapter One

WHAT KIND OF VIDEO?

The kind or style of video that you will make depends on your target audience — who are you making the video for?

For instance, is it for your own immediate family? Or will it be seen by distant relatives ... American or Australian 'cousins' perhaps?

Is it for a local history society with two potential audiences — the members themselves and members of the public who might view it at some local event?

Or is it intended to be seen by an entire community, such as the people who live in your village, or your colleagues at work?

The target audience inevitably dictates the style, shape and content of the completed video.

For instance, a local history society will be interested in documented information as well as views of the village, shots of buildings, and recorded reminiscences of senior citizens. Documented information could mean tools, medals and decorations, uniforms, working clothes, working skills and machinery, maps, wills, letters, public records such as Land Registry documents, Birth, Marriage and Death Certificates, sketches, paintings and old photographs, as well as relevant references in books and other publications.

A family video would be a much more personal record with more stress on interviews and old photographs and far less formally documented information. However, the clutter of a lived-in room is all part of the time capsule that you are recording and Grandpa's pipe rack on the wall, and those half dozen much smoked and chewed pipes may at first glance seem of no interest (because they are there in the background and have been for as long as one can remember), but they are part of his life and, as such, very relevant.

If the audience is a more general one, such as the people of your village or the local schoolchildren, the appeal must be more broadly based, painting with large strokes as it were, rather than dwelling on minute details.

Even the most popular home documentary *The Wedding* can benefit from this approach. If you're sending a copy to those distant cousins maybe you should tell them, with pictures, graphics or commentary, what the groom does for a living. Or maybe have an interview saying how they met.

What is the video trying to do? Having defined your audience you must now become even more specific in terms of the aim of the video.

For instance, is it intended to show some rare or dying craft or skill (or demonstrate a new skill as part of a company training scheme)?

Is it intended to capture 'family memories' to hand on to future generations, such as a christening or wedding?

Is it intended to recount the history of a village or community from 1066 to 1966?

Is the intention to gather statements from witnesses to an historical 'event' such as the Blitz or the day the factory closed and the town died?

Whatever the intention you need to be clear about it — write it down! Discuss it with friends and colleagues. And see if you can describe it in one paragraph! I used to say to budding television producers "if you can't write the 'programme billing' — that is, the short description of what is in your film — for *Radio Times* you can't make a programme!"

Once you have defined the aims and purpose of the video you will find that lots of things begin to fall into place. For instance the 'historical event' will be Interview led, that is to say the bulk of the video, the raw material, will be the recollections of people 'who were there'.

A video about a dying craft or about a new skill or technique, will need ample illustrations of the craft or technique itself, the tools that are used and the function of each tool, the various skills that are required, perhaps comparisons with modern materials and tools that have replaced the old skills.

The interview in this situation might be of lesser importance and might be replaced by a commentary based on information gathered during 'off the record' interviews with the craftsman in question.

A video about the family might be a mixture of interview and documentation...even home movies, and the documentation might include pictures from the family album. But think also of putting family memories in the context of general history, not just because it might make your video more interesting, but because it might help future generations measure the 'scale' of the family history against national or world events.

For instance, my father was born in 1897 and his life-span included the reigns of Queen Victoria, Edward VII, George V, Edward VIII, George VI and Elizabeth II.

9

He also lived during the Boer War, World War I, the Russian Revolution, the Spanish Civil War, World War II, the Chinese Revolution, the Korean War.

He saw the arrival of the motor car, the telephone, radio and television, the aeroplane, the jet engine, the nuclear bomb, the computer, the calculator and decimalisation.

He just missed out on the microwave oven and the fax machine, the Falklands Campaign, the Gulf War, the fall of the Berlin Wall.

Now you can see my father in an historical context and not just a boring date...born 1897.

What Kind of Video? — Summary

- Who is it for? — What is it trying to do?

- Define your audience. Define your objectives?

- Define the scale and balance of your main ingredients, e.g. long interviews or short anecdotes?

- Lots of historical facts or more 'colourful' information?

- Lots of documented 'evidence' or 'period' artefacts?

- A long and comprehensive historical record?

- Or a *pot-pourri* of family memories?

- An appetising introduction to the historically interesting place we live in?

- Or a demonstration of how to pitch a tent?

Chapter Two

PLANNING THE VIDEO

Once you have defined your audience and the aims and purpose of the video you can get down to the detailed planning of the project and here again I urge you to keep written notes on your discussions and research because these will form the basis of your first Draft Script!

List on paper the basic ingredients

Will it include interviews? If so write down the names of the people to be interviewed and the subject areas to be covered by them. Also make a note of where you plan to interview them.

Will it be in their home or place of work?

Will the venue of the interview be part of the 'context' of the video? Perhaps on the site of the factory that closed, or where the scout camp will be held, or where George and Mildred had their first date.

Don't forget that a person's home can be part of the context of the interview — wedding photographs on the mantelpiece, holiday souvenirs in the 'display cabinet' (remember them?).

Will the content of the interview imply references to other people living or dead? If so make a written note of this and consider including a shot (if living) or a photograph (if dead) of that person.

Will the content of the interview imply references to places or events? If so make a written note and consider including shots of these places or do-cumentation of the events (such as newspaper cuttings or holiday postcards).

Will the video need to put a person or place in a geographical context? For instance, will maps be needed or shots of the area, wide angle views of the village or street, a shot of the house with the deserted factory in the background?

Will there be demonstrations of skills? If so, who will be showing these skills to you and where will this demonstration take place?

Will you need to show its geographical context? (e.g. the milking parlour is some distance from the farmhouse, but right next to the field where the cows live).

Will you need to show other buildings or tools that are relevant to the skill being demonstrated?

Will you need to take shots of the modern equival-ent of the skill in question...if so, where and who will provide you with the information and the facilities?

Are there documents?

In the broadest sense of historical documentation are there maps, books, papers, photographs, old movies or artefacts that will help you illustrate your video or add verification to your interviews?

Artefacts, again in the broadest sense, could in-clude souvenirs, equipment, clothing, medals, sign-posts, machinery, buildings, tombstones, street furniture, (horse troughs, cobbles, gas lamps, etc).

Make a written list of all these, with the names and addresses of the people who can provide them. At the same time include an extra column or space in your notes regarding permissions.

In many circumstances permission may be needed to photograph a site or artefact and, in the case of documents, permission is required from the owner/copyright holder.

Make sure that you have *written* permission in all cases. Similarly, with your interview subjects make sure that you have their written consent to use their interview and other pictures you take for your video.

This may seem somewhat pedantic, but sometimes people give verbal permission then change their minds. Your video may be used in another context some years from now and the people in it may raise objections. The copyright laws are complicated, but a simple written permission transfers the necessary rights to you and protects you against any future litigation.

Are there locations? We've touched on these already in that a documentary about history also has a geographical context but it's worth writing down a list of all likely locations and putting them into two simple categories — exteriors and interiors.

By **exteriors** we mean literally anything 'outside' such as landscapes, vistas, streets, buildings, gardens, farmyards, orchards, churches, hotels, and so on.

Similarly, by **interiors** we mean anything indoors such as barns, stables, churches, kitchens, bedrooms, parlours, reception rooms, offices, workshops, discos.

Again, add to this list any other information that may be relevant, such as: who owns the property? Is permission required to a) shoot it, b) enter it? It would be a pity for your video to be delayed because you're serving time for trespass or breach of copyright!

Also, add any other information that you think might be useful such as 'facing south', 'dominates surrounding streets', 'a major landmark', 'can be seen on horizon at sunset', 'looks good after a shower' (cobbles?).

Don't forget other areas of useful comment such as 'slippery path', 'very dark milking shed', 'no electricity', 'uses oil lamps' and, of course, 'savage guard dog!'

Slippery path means wear your wellies and safeguard your equipment.

A dark milking shed means you'll need lights.

Uses oil lamps means you have no access to mains electricity and should make sure your batteries are well charged and that you have plenty of spares.

Your production file is beginning to take shape and by now you should have some useful pieces of paper defining your audience and the aims of the video; lists of potential participants, documentation and locations; notes about permissions you are likely to require; and some early but important considerations about safety.

The production team

If you haven't yet sorted out 'who does what', now is the time to do it when you have a pretty clear idea of the task ahead, but before you've started the actual production.

So let's make a list (television and video production is all about lists!) of the 'jobs' in our production and where appropriate I'll explain what that job would be called in the TV and video Industry.

Bear in mind that one person can do more than one job and in fact there is a lot to be said for a very small team of three or four people rather than the entire membership of your local history society crowding into Grandpa Smith's caravan. If you are covering your sister's wedding it could be that it's you and your camcorder and you are wearing all the hats I am going to describe. It's still useful for you to be aware of the various job descriptions even if it's just a reminder of all the things to be done.

Camera Operator
Obviously essential and this one person might also cover **sound** and **lighting** with other members of the team being 'helpers'.

15

Researcher
As vital as the camera operator. No research, no video. The researcher would keep notes on interviewees, related documents and artefacts, and might also assume responsibilty for permissions. The vicar may not allow filming inside the church or during the ceremony...find out in advance and avoid tears on the day.

Another possible role for the researcher might be that of the **interviewer**, the logic being that someone who is most knowledgable in a subject area is best suited to ask questions about it.

Director
A director in the television or video industry is responsible for the 'shots' that we see and for the 'performances'. And it is the director who decides the final 'shape' of the film or video (and therefore supervises the editing and all post-production work such as music, titles and commentary).

This could be the researcher or the camera operator but there is a lot to be said for having one person specifically charged with the task of keeping an 'overview' of the project whilst other team members concentrate on their own particular area of responsibility.

Interviewer
As suggested earlier, this could be an additional task for the researcher, but there could well be someone within your group who has a particular talent for 'drawing people out of themselves' and extracting those elusive gems of anecdote and information. If you are doing a film about your village, or workplace, or your family history, someone who may already have some experience of oral history might be well suited to the job. And, of course, the interviewer does not have to be 'on board' the project all the time.

Notetaker!
One of the most important jobs in the television and video industry is that of production assistant or director's assistant, and in television drama and the feature film industry the post is subdivided so that one person specialises in continuity — a very specialist area.

But for our purposes the notetaker is closer to the TV production assistant and the duties include:

- Keeping details of contributors and locations.

- Listing every shot on location. Making notes of the broad content of the interview and, from these notes, helping the director to decide if other shots should be taken of any relevant documents or artefacts (cutaways).

- Helping the director prepare the Draft Script, the Shooting Script, and the Editing Script.

- Helping the editor find shots when the first assembly is taking place (the Rough Cut).

'The director ... decides the final shape of the video'

- With the researcher, obtaining clearances and permissions. (If your team is very small perhaps the director could also take on this role).

Editor
This is the person who joins all the shots together and adds commentaries, titles and music. Like the camera operator some familiarity with knobs and buttons is useful and it could well be that the camera operator is also the editor.

Planning the Video — Summary

- Put your basic ingredients on paper.

- List possible interviewees and where the interviews will take place.

- Will the interview location be itself of historical relevance?

- Is there a geographical relevance as well?

- List possible references to places or events.

- List demonstrations of skills, where these will happen and relevant tools.

- Is a modern comparison required and who can provide this?

- List your locations, exteriors and interiors with notes.

- Make a list of the permissions you are likely to need.

- Decide who does what.

- Start thinking safety!

Chapter Three

THE RECCE

Let's say our project is aimed at our local history society as a primary audience, but that it could also be shown in the local school.

Let's say the aim of the video is to show how a local farmer and his wife milk their herd of dairy cows by hand — not perhaps a dying skill, but certainly one that invites interesting comparisons with the more usual machine milking process.

Our list of ingredients includes shots of the village and of the farm. We know the farmer has photographs going back some years that are of interest, and we plan to interview the farmer and his wife and also show the hand milking process.

We've defined who does what, so we are ready for the recce. Members of the group may already be familiar with the farm and the farmer and his wife, so you may feel you don't need a reconnaissance or recce. Wrong!

The recce is vital. You will be visiting the farm on a formal basis this time, no matter how informal your actual relationship may be.

You will be looking at things in an entirely different light.

You will be working together as a team, thinking ahead to how your filming is going to work out in the various locations.

And you'll be making lists again!!

Take a new look at the village High Street with your video project in mind and various things begin to emerge.

As you look up the High Street you suddenly realise that it is criss-crossed with telephone and electric cables...so make a note to tighten the shot, or lose some of the sky to avoid these.

'... the High Street is criss-crossed with telephone wires ...'

The church with its beautiful tower is the heart of the village. But the tower is being renovated and is surrounded by scaffolding. Make a note to find out when the scaffolding will have gone and maybe shoot the church later in the year.

Make arrangements with the farmer to visit him at a convenient time — convenient for him that is! Alllow plenty of time for this formal recce and make sure that the farmer is well aware of this. Not only is it rude to have glibly mentioned half an hour and then stay for half a day — it will not give him much confidence in you as a production team.

So be honest with him. Explain that you would like to describe your project to him and his wife and discuss the history of the farm and hand milking so that you can prepare the interviews and not waste his time later on. Ask if he could spare the time to show you round the farm and especially the milking area. And warn him that you would also like to look at any maps or photographs that they might have available as possible ingredients in your video.

Make sure he is happy about the number of people who will visit him on the recce. The director is essential, so is the researcher or interviewer because of the historical nature of the project. But a Press Gang of five or six might be a bit off-putting for him.

Finally, tell him how many cars you might be bringing to the recce and make sure he is happy about this...the whole project could collapse if a fleet of vehicles blocks his driveway and delays a vital delivery of farm supplies!

Once it's all agreed assemble your recce team, make sure you have suitable clothing, notepads (for your lists!), a cassette recorder (more on that later), and if it's a time-consuming recce take cups and a Thermos of tea, and two spare cups for the farmer and his wife — they'll appreciate the gesture!

Now you're at the farm and, as I said earlier sit down with the farmer and his wife and explain the project to them. Who is going to see the completed video, why you are making the video, and their role in it.

Make it clear to them that they will have total control over their input and over their portrayal in the final video. So if they say something that they wished they hadn't said, make it clear that you will remove that section or replace it with something with which they will be comfortable.

We're really saying 'no skeletons from your cup-boards' and people will welcome this form of re-as-surance. Make them feel that they will have control over their input and that they are the experts. You're saying and doing all this to put them at their ease so that when shooting begins they will be relaxed and the interviews will flow!

Next discuss with them the kind of information you hope will emerge during the interviews...how long they have been on the farm, when they got mar-ried, the development of the herd (breeding pro-grammes, for instance), and why they choose to milk by hand.

As this informal discussion develops you will realise that information is pouring out and you may well consider asking their permission to use a small tape recorder. This has two advantages: firstly, you can play it back later and get a clearer idea of the

'... make them feel that they will have control over their input ...'

content of the interviews which will help you 'shape' them and, secondly, the couple will become used to a technical 'object' being around.

For some reason people who are being interviewed find the microphone more daunting than the camera, maybe because they are more nervous about speaking in public than about being photographed, so a small cassette recorder at this first visit might be a gentle way to 'break them in'.

Without being 'nosey' look around the room or rooms where your discussion is taking place and make a note of what you see. You will almost certainly find plenty of cutaways and now might be the time to get technical for a while.

Cutaways

Cutaways are the nuts and bolts of film, television and video production in that, like nuts and bolts, they are part of the joining together process.

In television news programmes you will see interviews with politicians, and every now and then a brief shot of the reporter, often nodding. This is a 'cutaway' shot of the reporter, that is a cutaway from the main film to something or somebody else. In news programmes these cutaways of the reporters (or 'Noddies' as they are called) are used to shorten or edit the interview. The nodding reporter hides the join! Without a cutaway the politician would appear to jerk or leap about the screen as one shot is joined to the next.

In documentary programmes cutaways are not so much used to hide a join as to give you additional information and these are the kinds of cutaways we will be using in our video.

For instance, the farmer in the interview may refer to his wife "She's much better at hand milking than me!". That's where you might consider 'cutting away to' his wife sitting alongside him or edit in a shot of his wife milking.

You wouldn't stop filming the farmer to do this, you would wait until the interview was over and take a shot of the farmer's wife, beaming smugly perhaps!

This is a **direct** cutaway triggered logically by the farmer's reference to his wife.

Another **direct** cutaway might be a complete **sequence** of shots. For instance if the farmer were to say "I bring the cows in from pasture at first light" your viewers might expect to see that. And it would be on one of your lists wouldn't it?!

However there are what I call **indirect** cutaways that do not detract or distract from the content of the interview but enhance the viewer's understanding of the farmer and his wife.

For instance, she might rotate her wedding ring round her finger when she is listening to her husband — one of her characteristic gestures.

The farmer might tamp down the tobacco in his pipe as he talks. This would make a nice cutaway.

And the house itself could be a mine of cutaways.

We stamp our lives, our personalities and our personal histories on our homes.

If we are effectively to convey to the viewer the 'character' of the farmer, as well as the content of his interview, his home and workplace will offer many cutaways that will help us build up a richer and more descriptive picture of the man. So:

- Look at the walls for paintings, pictures, photographs, lamps, clocks, even plants in pots.

- Look at the shelves for books, souvenirs, bric-à-brac.

- Look at the furniture and furnishings, everything you see is part of the mosaic of this man.

Back at the recce

You've now made copious notes about cutaways and you're beginning to get a clearer idea of the ground to be covered when you shoot the interviews.

Move on now with the farmer and his wife to the farmyard so they can talk you through their daily routine. Again, look around for cutaways that will enhance your viewer's understanding and appreciation of the farm.

If you have the tape recorder keep it running because as the farmer and his wife relax on home ground more gems of information will emerge. That was one there! That came as a surprise...that the farm was actually the *first* in the area to introduce mechanical milking. So why did they go back to hand milking?

Towards the end of the recce you'll have built up a list of interview locations, demonstration locations, cutaways, and other shots that you will need.

Hopefully you will also have been making notes about electricity supplies for your lights (if you have them) and camera, and of those areas where you will only be battery-powered, and notes about areas that might be cramped, noisy, dark, dangerous or wet!

Back at the farmhouse confirm with the farmer that these are the locations you have in mind unless he objects or has a better idea.

Confirm also what documents or photographs he can provide for the project and, if you are taking them away to shoot in advance of filming or to mount them on card before shooting starts, *assure* him that they will be returned in good condition.

Finally, agree on shooting times and dates, ask the farmer about any special safety requirements, any permissions that might be needed (e.g. to put the camera on adjoining land to take your long shot of the farm), and agree on parking arrangements.

The Recce — Summary

- The recce is VITAL.

- Take a fresh look at your locations.

- Allow plenty of time.

- Take notes and maybe a tape recorder.

- Re-assure your interviewees — they have control.

- Look out for cutaways.

- Check out electric points, dark areas, etc.

- Take care of other people's possessions.

- Be safe and have permission.

- Confirm dates and times.

- Take your own tea!

Chapter Four

DRAFT SCRIPT

Now we've completed the recce and taken copious notes let's firm up on the very broad schedule
that was shaping up before and at the recce and,
at the same time, let's revise our outline ideas about
the structure or shape of the final video.

The shape of the final video

We will probably want it to begin with some views
of the village whilst a commentary, which is recorded separately and added to the video, tells us
where we are and gives us some information, both
historical and geographical about the village.

We might make a side note about a map being
useful here as well, and perhaps a shot of the
signpost in the middle of the village that says Rugby
10 miles, Daventry 3 miles, and Northampton 12
miles. Plus of, course, old paintings of the village, the
kind of mention it got in the Domesday Book, etc.

Then, perhaps, we move to the farm and again
place it in a geographical and historical context
before we meet the farmer and his wife and hear
from them about their life together and how the
farm developed over the years.

Milking time might be the next sequence and we
should consider visiting another dairy farm to look
at the mechanical milking process before returning
to our farmer and his wife for some final words,
perhaps about how they see the future of hand
milking.

'... We will probably want the video to begin with some
views of the village ...'

Notice that I've described the entire video in a few
paragraphs, painting with very broad brush strokes
the general 'shape' of the finished video.

Notice also that I used the word **sequence** which is
a specialised word in the television industry and one
that will be useful for you with your project.

A sequence is a series of related shots joined
together to make a 'stand-alone' segment within a
film or programme.

We all know that a film is a series of shots, joined
together and following one after the other until the

end titles. But in a feature film we are talking about thousands of shots and this is a daunting and per- haps difficult concept to cope with if we are setting out to make our first documentary.

If, however, we think of a film as being made up of sequences, we go from thousands to a few and, in the case of our project, maybe four or five. With this we can cope!

Once we've broken our project into digestible se- quences we can go into more detail within each sequence, even to nominating individual shots be- cause they are particularly important.

Very quickly this draft shape is beginning to turn into a Draft Script, a fairly detailed description of the finished project. When you've filmed everything and edited it all together, the video may be quite different but at least a Draft Script gives you a framework within which you can work. And it's only a piece of paper...you can modify it, add to it, cut things out as your project proceeds.

On the next page I've given you a sample Draft Script to look at, but don't feel obliged to use that format. As long as you have a method of showing what's next any format will do. With experience, everyone arrives at their own way of scripting.

By the way the cynical reader may notice that a Draft Script is really a complicated list!

Notes about the Draft Script

Sequences can be a-z or 1-100 but I prefer letters for sequences and numbers for shots.

I have also given each sequence a short descrip- tive title.

DRAFT SCRIPT

Seq	Shot	Picture	Source	Sound	Location	Notes
A **Titles**	1	Title "Hand Milking in West Haddon"	Jim	Music	Study	
	2	Title "A Local History Project"				
B **Intro to Village**	3	LS Village		VO	Ext.	
	4	High Street				
	5	Church				
	6	Domesday Book	Mary			
	7	Map	Mary			
C **Intro to Farm**	8	LS Farm		No VO	Ext.	
	9	Farm House				
	10	Mr & Mrs at door				
D **Re Hand Milking**	11	Interview Mr			Kitchen	
	12	Cutaways Utensils				
	13	C/way Mrs				
	14	C/way cat				
E **Hand Milking**	15	LS Cows		VO	Ext.	
	16	Milking Shed				
	17	C/ways Utensils on walls				
F **History of Farm**	18	Interview Mrs			Parlour	
	19	Cutaways pictures				
	20	Cutaways photos				
G **Mechanical**	21	Modern machine milking shed			Int.	Lights!

The picture is a brief description of the shot and notice some television jargon or shorthand creeping in here:

LS = Long Shot or Wide Angle or View or Vista!
VO = Voice Over or Commentary
Ext = Exterior so, hopefully,no lights are needed.

Source means 'where is it coming from?' and in this case Jim is making the titles for us with his Letraset and cardboard and Mary, our researcher, is providing the Domesday Book reference and a map.

Notice that I have grouped cutaways under one shot number because at this stage we only know there will be cutaways not how many there will be.

Once you are on location you can use one shot number for 'kitchen pans', and another for 'farm cats' or number them individually...particularly if you wish to identify a photograph of someone who has been mentioned in an interview.

Also your location shot numbers will be quite different numbers (more of this later) but if 'Interview Mr' is Shot 143 on location you can write 143 opposite Sequence **D** Shot 11 on your Draft Script and you'll know where you are.

You may find that you scrawl extra notes on the Draft Script as new ideas or alternatives strike you. Fine, as long as you can understand it, do it your own way.

The **notes** column can be used as a reminder column (e.g. no electricity in kitchen).

Notice that I've used double spacing. It is probably better to use treble spacing so that as you go along you have plenty of space for extra notes and reminders.

Draft Script — Summary

- Sketch out a broad 'shape' for your video.

- Think in 'sequences' such as village, farm, milking time.

- Make notes of 'Sources' (who's getting the map?)

- Make notes of 'blocks' of cutaways (cats, kitchen pans).

- Identify each sequence with a number or letter.

- Leave space for notes (no power point in barn).

Chapter Five

SHOOTING SCRIPT & SHOOTING SCHEDULE

The Draft Script is our Grand Plan and it now forms the basis of the rest of the production through shooting and editing and on to commentary and any titles that might be added.

You will find that you are constantly referring to it, adding and adjusting here and there but using it always as your prime reference. It is now going to form the basis of our Shooting Schedule and our Shooting Script.

We need a Shooting Schedule for several reasons:

- It is courteous to the people we are filming and avoids wasting their time.

- It helps us make the best use of our time and of our resources, such as equipment, extra help, and so on.

- It gives us a flexible framework so that if it rains we can shoot something inside.

- It serves as a handy reminder list. For instance, a music stand makes a good caption stand if you are going to shoot photographs. You'll need to mount them temporarily on stiff card, Blu-tack is useful for this. So a reminder list at the end of the Schedule can save you a lot of time on location.

First, we look at our Draft Script sequence by sequence and see which sequences we will be shooting in one location.

So clearly the farm and the farmer and his wife leap out at us as being one location.

Then we break this down by sequences again to sub-locations.

SHOOTING SCHEDULE

Day One

Morning	Interview Farmer	Sequence D	Int.
Afternoon	Interview Mrs F	Sequence F	Int.

Day Two

Morning	Milking	Sequence E	Ext. & Int.
Afternoon	The Farm	Sequence C (Need Mr & Mrs for Shot 10, same clothes as Day 1	Ext.

Day Three

Morning	Machine Milking	Sequence G	(Lights) Interior & Exterior
Afternoon	The Village	Sequence B	Ext.

Day Four

Morning	The Farm	Sequence H	Ext.
Afternoon	Extra Shots		

Day Five

All Day Shoot —Maps, Photographs and Titles at Jim's House. Borrow Music Stand from Sally's daughter. Remember Blu-Tack!

Then we break it down again to cover interiors, exteriors, and cutaways.

Have a look at a possible schedule below:

Notice that I've started with the main interviews. The reason for this is that you will have a clearer idea of cutaways, other interviews, the sequences about mechanical milking and so on, when you have heard what Mr and Mrs F actually say in their interviews.

As these interviews are interiors you have no weather problems so if you get through Day One the 'core' of your video is already 'in the can'!

Once we have this broad Shooting Schedule we can compile a more detailed one for each Shooting Day as follows:

Day One	Date.....	Time....	Location
	1.12.94	10.00	The Farm

1 car to be parked in driveway. NB Do not block entry to barn. Director bringing coffee and biscuits.

10.15 Set up camera in kitchen (may need lights).

10.30 Talk to farmer about interview.

11.00 Shoot Interview (Sequence D shot 11) and any relevant cutaways of Mr.F (twiddling his thumbs?).

11.30 Coffee break.

12.00 Shoot Mrs F listening (D/13) Kitchen utensils (D/12). The cat (D/14).
Arrange with Mr and Mrs F to leave gear in porch.

13.00 Lunch at Pub in village.

35

14.15 Return to farm

14.30 Set up camera in parlour. (Good light from window so could seat Mrs F. at table in window bay).

14.45 Talk to Mrs F about Interview.

15.00 Shoot Interview (Sequence F Shot 18). Shoot any relevant cutaways of Mrs F (her wedding ring?).

15.30 Tea break.

16.00 Shoot pictures on walls of parlour (F/19) Shoot photos on walls and shelves (F/20). (Lights will be needed).

16.30 Parcel up any pictures and maps, etc that Mr and Mrs F will be lending for possible inclusion in the video.

Give Mr and Mrs F an itemised receipt for these. Ask Mr and Mrs F to sign permission agreements for you to use their interviews and cutaways in your video.

17.00 Collect all gear, tidy up and depart.

Schedule parameters

Notice that both the schedules so far are still basically 'lists' but there are simple ground rules or parameters that should be applied to make life easier for everyone and to make your shooting schedules as efficient as possible.

Don't feel obliged to shoot in sequence, i.e. don't try and shoot Shot 1 of your Draft Script, then Shot 2 and so on, because you'll be running around all over the place.

That's why your Main Shooting Schedule is broken down into Main Locations such as the village, the farm, etc.

That's why your Daily Shooting Schedule is broken down even further so that all the milking parlour shots are done at the same time.

You'll find that the 'shoot' itself just takes a few minutes. It's the setting-up of lights, tripod, camera, microphone and so on that is really time consuming.

Shoot in the same direction

You can break your Daily Shooting Schedule down even further, for instance, if you are taking shots of paintings and photographs in a room...shoot them wall by wall!

They won't be in the right order for your final video but that's what editing is all about.

So think about organising your schedules in general terms to begin with: e.g. general exteriors with and without the farmer in shot.

- Exterior interviews and related cutaways.

- Interior interviews and related cutaways.

- Sound only interviews and sound tracks (machinery noises, for instance).

- Cutaways that are not located at sites of interviews and demonstrations.

Then:

Look at this in the light of camera and equipment movement and send a simple version of it to the farmer for his approval.

Shooting Script — Summary

- Plan the structure of the final video.

- Think of it as 'sequences'.

- Prepare a Draft Script.

- From this prepare a Shooting Schedule.

- From this prepare a Daily Schedule or Shooting Script.

- Shoot out of sequence to minimise setting-up times.

- Shoot in the same direction.

- Make sure your contributors are happy with the Shooting Schedule.

Chapter Six

THE INTERVIEW

Now our various schedules are in place, and before the actual 'shoot' starts let's spend a few minutes thinking about the core material of the video.

Interviews are about getting fluent 'batches' of well-shaped information. So you must define the broad subject area of each interview and make sure that the interviewee understands and agrees with your thinking on this.

You must put the interviewee at ease so that you can draw out this information in a natural and relaxed way.

You must agree in advance a shape or structure for the interview (even if it is as simple as a chronological blow-by-blow account of an event).

You must be prepared to pursue an interesting digression.

You must be ready to 'get back on course' after a digression.

In addition, you must decide now what 'style' of interview you want to record. For instance, do you wish to see and hear the interviewer in the finished video? If so, there are tremendous implications for the Shooting Schedule because you will need an extra microphone for the interviewer, and also cutaways of the interviewer asking the questions, nodding at the replies, looking at photographs or handling artefacts.

Do you wish *only* to hear the interviewer asking the questions? (i.e. to hear his/her question but not see the interviewer).

If so why? Could not this be replaced in commentary? e.g. "But why does Mr Farmer prefer hand-milking?"

Are you aiming for 'seamless' flows of information? If so, how will they be seamless? Will you train and coax our interviewee to 'speak paragraphs'?

Or will you cover the joins with pictures of the contributor going about his business? If so, will the pictures be relevant and enhancing or will they be irrelevant and distracting?

Decisions! Decisions!

Some interview tips

The double interview
Do a short interview that covers the main points in almost headline terms. This relaxes both the interviewer and the interviewee. It places subconscious headings in the mind of the interviewee so that he or she is more likely to be 'in sync' with you later.

"Yes, the uncle Henry who eloped with the vicar's daughter!"

It sometimes gives advance warning of some mineable little digression that could be pure gold.

It gives you the chance to correct any little irritations such as swivelling in a swivel chair. (Get rid of it).

It gives you the chance to refer back to something that was said so that you'll get a complete paragraph.

"Tell me about the member of your family who eloped."

"Tell me how you and Jenny first met."

"Just remind me of why it is so important always to install a new gasket."

The W question
If you ask a question such as "Did you do National Service?", you'll get a "Yes" or a "No" answer.

So try and use "Why?", Where?", "Who?", "What?"

"What did you feel about National Service?"

No one can answer that question with a "Yes" or "No!"

"Why should we pitch our tents at the top of the hill?"

"Where did you and Jenny meet?"

The pause
Be brave and sit silently rather than crash in with the next question. So often the 'gem' is in the second paragraph and you tease this out with a silence.

The interviewee always 'cracks' first — certainly in my experience, anyway.

Short questions are better than long questions

Questions later in the interview
These tend to receive 'better' replies than earlier questions. (Hence the double interview as an alternative).

LISTEN!
Your next question may be irrelevant or unnecessary.

BE QUIET!
Keep eyeball to eyeball contact with your interviewee and nod and smile encouragingly — but DO NOT keep saying "Yes" or "Ah, Ah" or "Mmmm". It'll ruin your sound track and make editing difficult if not impossible.

If you decide that you really want to have pictures of the interviewer asking questions (and nodding!) make a note of the questions so that you can re-shoot them separately when you have completed the main interview. The interviewee may have left the room to go about some business, so get a colleague to sit in the same position as the interviewee and look at you so that the 'eyelines' look right.

Interview — Summary

- Aim for fluent 'batches' of information.

- Interviewee 'in the picture' re content.

- Interviewee at ease.

- Structure in advance.

- Pursue interesting digressions.

- Interviewer in vision? In sound?

- Consider short followed by long interview.

- Who, What, Where, When, Why? (and How?).

- Sit out the silences.

- Listen!

- Be quiet!

- Re-shoot questions and 'noddies'.

Chapter Seven

EQUIPMENT

Obviously you have a camera with either a built-in recording facility (a camcorder), or a camera that can be attached to a separate recorder.

You will have a microphone as part of the structure of the camera (an integral mic), or some means of attaching a microphone to your recorder. You may even have the facility to plug an additional microphone or microphones into your camcorder.

You will also have some form of cassette to fit your camcorder or video recorder.

These are the basics...picture, sound and tape.

But we should add two more vital pieces of equipment and consider one or two others.

Tripod
A tripod is vital because it is a steady camera platform and nothing is more distracting than an unsteady shot.

Also, if you must pan or zoom (and I have strong reservations about panning and zooming), then at least the tripod will add lateral or vertical smoothness to your shot.

Lights
You are sure to need some form of additional lighting but do remember that the camera-mounted 'headlamp' that comes with some camcorders is not necessarily the best method of improving your picture.

Additional Equipment

In my view equally vital:
A clapperboard! — Yes, just like they use in the movies. The clapperboard originated as a means of identifying a shot *and* synchronising the sound. If the film editor 'lined up' the sharp Whack of the sound track as the upper segment of the board clapped down on to the lower segment with the picture frame of the point of impact then sound and vision would be perfectly parallel or synchronous (in sync).

With a video camera you are recording sound and picture on the same tape and you are automatically in sync. But a clapperboard is a wonderfully easy way of identifying each shot and giving you other information as well. Information that is useful on location and at the editing stage.

You can write on it '1' meaning cassette 1; '1' meaning Shot 1; '3' meaning the third version of shot 1.

So if your notetaker is carefully noting what is on each board before each shot you will know that the above shot can be found on Cassette 1, and is marked 1/1/3 because it is the third 'take' of Shot One.

You don't have to buy a proper clapperboard and you don't have to 'clap' it. A piece of card and a felt tip pen, or a message board with those pens that leave a message that can be wiped off with a damp cloth will do the job.

It will save you *hours* of time at the editing stage.

Note: Some of the more sophisticated cameras offer a facility called time coding. This burns in the time of day on one of the tracks on your tape. So if

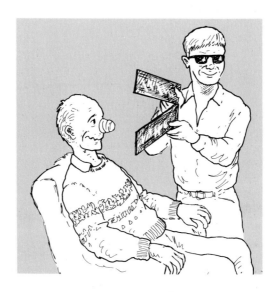

'... You don't have to buy a proper clapperboard and
you don't *have* to 'clap' it ...'

Jenny said 'I do!' at 11.37 you can spool through to
11.37 on the tape and there she is. More on this at
the editing stage.

Consider also:
A wheelchair — wonderful for tracking shots! Water-
proof cases of some kind for cassettes. Brollies and
wellies. Thermos flasks of tea and coffee. Plastic
bags for your rubbish. Additional mics (more on that
later). Separate tape recorder (ditto). Reflectors
(more under *Lighting*) A portable TV monitor (a
luxury but marvellous for double-checking 'framing' before you shoot.)

Blu-Tack, masking-tape, double-sided Sellotape,
pens, notebooks, 'permission' papers. Sticky labels
for cassettes and 'things you borrow'. Plastic bags
and envelopes for 'things you borrow'.

Equipment — Summary

- Camera, recorder, microphone, tapes.
- Tripod.
- Lights.
- Clapperboard/blackboard.
- TV monitor.
- Wheelchair.
- Brollies and wellies.
- Plastic bags for rubbish, cassettes, artefacts, photos.
- Blu-tack, labels, sticky tapes.
- Permission papers.
- Paper and pencils.

Chapter Eight

SHOOTING TIPS

Use a Tripod

The best tip I can give you is to use a tripod — that way your shots will be steady and watchable.

Try and find the biggest and heaviest tripod available. It's a pain to carry around but it really is worth it. Try and find one with a spirit level built into the panning head so that your horizons are horizontal.

Try and find one with a pan and tilt head that can be firmly locked, but also, should you need to pan or tilt whilst you are shooting, check the 'friction' of the pan and tilt movement so that it offers a controllable resistance as you move it, rather than loosely wobbling all over the place.

Shoot static shots

Next be careful to shoot 'static' shots most of the time. Pans or zooms or 'focus-pulls' (where the foreground is blurred and the background sharp, and then the foreground turns into a rose with a drop of rainwater on it and the background goes all blurred?) have their place and by all means experiment. But remember that our objective is to capture and assemble visual and aural information in a way that is clear to the viewer/listener and without distractions.

So put the camera on the tripod, frame the shot and shoot.

'...the more filmatic we become, the more
we understand our own authority ...'

The more 'filmatic' we become the more we under-
mine our own authority. Our video should say:

Village, farm, farmhouse, farmer, farmyard, field,
cows.

NOT: Autumn sunset, pretty thatch, gnarled yokel,
windswept paddock, Van Gogh field, lowing bo-
vines.

We are capturing raw material here and we can all
too easily invalidate the authenticity of that material at the shooting stage and also at the editing
stage if we indulge in frills and trickeries.

So put the camera on the tripod, frame the shot,
and shoot.

Frame the shot

There is no need to go into the precise business of shot sizes as defined by various sections of the film and television industries such as Medium Long Shot, Big Close Up, etc, but it is useful to know what the basic shot sizes are called even if it just helps communication between director and camera operator or director and editor.

I was recently on location with a TV company and a reporter was yelling at the videotape editor saying "I definitely took a close-up of that athlete". The editor kept saying he couldn't find a close-up.

In the event, there were two shots of the athlete in question. The first showed the entire stadium (and he was in there somewhere), and the second showed six athletes full length...and our man was the one in the middle!

The standard shots are:

Medium Close Up (MCU) which is the face or head and shoulders. It's the shot you see all the time on the television. Close Up and Big Close Up are really for drama.

Mid Shot (MS). Head and torso, cutting at the waist. The kind of shot size in which there are two people in the shot, or which shows the hands, or someone is holding something that's relevant to the interview such as a prize piglet.

Long Shot (LS). That's the entire body from head to toe, including the bride's train!

Wide Shot (WS). The 'scene setter'. It can be the village high street, the church, the church porch with *all* the guests, the factory, the farmyard.

Medium close-up
(MCU) ...

Mid-shot
(MS)

Long shot
(LS)

When to use what?

The basic rule is to start wide (show the church), and then go progressively tighter (to draw your viewer into the scene). So, WS church. A closer WS porch and guests. LS bride and groom wearing their smart outfits. MS bride with bouquet. MCU smiling bride with pretty veil and pearl necklace.

A basic rule with 'talking heads' is to keep the same shot size, otherwise you get sea-sick when you join lots of shots together. So a cut from Grandpa MCU (head and shoulders) to Grandma MCU will work just fine. Grandma in LS would only work if there were a reason for the long shot (e.g. she's showing us her kitchen). Always try and visualize how a shot might look.

All you need to ask yourself as you look in the viewfinder is "Does this shot contain the information I want to show to the viewer?"

If it does — that's your shot!

But look at it very carefully because it might also contain information that you don't want to be seen, or something that is irrelevant or distracting.

With exteriors watch out for electricity pylons and telephone lines.

With interiors watch out for 'clutter' such as a pile of washing in the background, cables to 'phones and TV sets that could be tidied up a bit — not because you wish to falsify the image but because they could be terribly distracting when the video is finally viewed.

Instinctively you will be looking at the centre of the picture. But look around the edges, at the sides and the top and bottom of the frame.

Will a shot carry more authenticity by being a little wider to include artefacts on a foreground desk, pictures on a wall, or will these intrude and be best used as cutaways?

Or should there be *two* shots? One that includes 'the environment' of the interview and then a closer shot that only contains the interviewee?

Although it is an additional piece of equipment to carry around with related problems such as cables and batteries, etc, a TV monitor attached to the camera can be very useful in checking out the shot, particularly for interiors and when lights are being used.

It is much easier to spot odd colours (because your camera has not been 'set' correctly for artificial lights), flare from reflected lights, and untidy edges around the shot.

Zooms and Pans

From the great importance I have attached to static shots you will have gathered that I have strong reservations about zooms and pans, yet there I am suggesting that a wheelchair can be useful for tracking shots!

There is a big technical difference between a zoom and a track and a definition of the two words will help you understand.

A *zoom* is a sequence of still photographs (Yes it is!) that apparently approach or retreat from the centre of interest by physically changing the characteristics of the lens. In other words if you start with the entire field and zoom into the cow your lens is a wide angle lens at the start of the shot and a telephoto lens at the end of the shot, and at each stage of the zoom the lens has the characteristics of whatever lens it thinks it is.

Say there is a barn twenty actual feet behind the cow. Because a wide angle lens increases apparent distances the barn, at the start of the zoom, will appear to be sixty feet behind the cow. Because a telephoto lens compresses apparent distances the barn, at the end of the zoom, will appear to be three feet behind the cow.

So as we zoom, the foreground, background and edges of the shot are undergoing a massive range of visual/perspective distortions.

Very distracting!

A *tracking shot* uses a fixed lens (if your camcorder has a zoom then you set your zoom at a 'natural' angle, not quite at the widest wide-angle, and leave it alone).

You can then track forwards to the cow and the apparent distance between the cow and the shed will remain the same.

The edges of the shot will change, but in a natural way not in an optically distorted way.

You can also track 'sideways' with a fixed lens, for instance, if your wheelchair is moving parallel to a racehorse!

Tip! The closer your lens is to a telephoto setting the more likely it is to wobble and judder.

Panning and tilting

Panning means the camera moves from left to right or vice versa.

Tilting means the camera moves from down to up or vice versa. (You can't pan up or down because pan(orama) refers to width not height!).

A *pan* is a series of still shots (Yes it is!) that goes from left to right or right to left.

Why would you use a pan?

Normally you would use a pan because you are following a movement (cow crosses farmyard and enters cowshed). in this case the cow's movement motivates or justifies the pan.

People often use a pan to indicate a vista or a big 'view'. They may have been influenced by watching Westerns and the big pan across the landscape. Everything in the picture saying 'big'.

But if you look carefully at those big pans in the Westerns you'll find they are normally just as motivated as my suggestion that you pan the cow across the farmyard. If you look carefully or search your memory, you'll see or recall that the pan is there because there is a lone horseman in the distance, riding left to right across the plain or approaching the camera.

My rule of thumb is: if you want to say 'big', shoot wide and static. Use a pan only if you can justify using it.

In really Big Country your pan is actually a series of wide shots...how else would you show *Oklahoma*? But a farm?

So pan if it is properly motivated (and remember how wobbly the telephoto end of the zoom will be), and leave 'space' to the left if you are panning left, or right if you are panning right so that we know where the cow is heading.

(Always leave space left or right of frame in static as well as panning shots if 'looking' or movement or direction is suggested...a nose rammed up against the side of the telly and a big space behind the back of the interviewee's head looks wrong!).

Tilting

I have similar reservations about tilting. Following a parachutist from aeroplane to ground can be justified. Tilting from church tower to church porch cannot be justified. Better to show all the church, then the tower (if it is significant), then the porch.

Tip! When in doubt concerning a pan or a tilt think what your own eyes are actually doing. Following that racehorse they will be going click click click at amazing speed (a series of stills that your brain calls a pan). Studying the church they will go click church click tower click Clock click porch. Try it!

Lens characteristics

Don't panic! We're not going to get too technical but having warned you about telephoto shots being wobbly, a couple of minutes on how you can use these characteristics to your advantage will be time well spent.

Wide angle
This end of the zoom lens is larger than life and distorts *outwards*. It can make a small office look big. It's safe for shots when the camera is moving as it decreases apparent camera shake. It's handy if you can't step backwards any further to get that shot of the house, village hall, village choir, wedding group, etc.

But be careful if you use it at close quarters, such as an interview, as it distorts the foreground. So, depending on the framing of the shot, your interviewee could end up with an enormous chin or nose, or the foreground desk might appear to be half an acre in area with giant inkwells and *Gulliver's Travels* telephones.

Telephoto
This end of the zoom lens distorts *inwards* so the hurdles on an athletics track appear to be only a few inches apart. It's unsafe for shots with camera movement as it increases apparent camera shake.

If you want to make a city's rush hour traffic look really busy use a telephoto lens...the compression effect will be dramatic with just a few cars. Dramatic. Yes! But accurate? Authentic? Verifiable? No!

But if you can't cross that ravine and really need the shot of the log cabin, or you cannot move around the church during the service but need a shot of the vicar, then the telephoto end of the lens has its uses...on a tripod.

Standard
This is a lens, or the setting on a zoom, that is closest

VIDEO DOCUMENTARY MAKING

to how we think reality is. (Our brain's perception of reality and reality itself are actually quite different things, but that's another book).

It's when the barn is thirty feet behind the cow and when we look at the shot we still think the barn is thirty feet behind the cow.

My advice is to be aware of the risk of distortions with the extreme 'ends' of the zoom lens and tuck this away at the back of your mind. Shoot static shots rather than zoom and pan, otherwise you'll have trouble editing it all together.

Shooting Tips — Summary

- Use a tripod.

- Shoot static shots.

- Avoid clutter.

- Track rather than zoom.

- Motivate your pans.

- Echo what your eyes do.

- Leave looking room and walking room.

- Beware of telephoto judder.

- A TV monitor can help with framing.

- Look at the top and sides of the shot as well as in the middle of the viewfinder.

Chapter Nine

THE PRACTICE SHOOT

If you are planning to make a documentary of any kind, whether it's about our hand milking farmer or a school outing or some new work methods in the factory or office set aside half a day to do a practice shoot.

You may be familiar with your camera and other equipment but this is the first time you will be working as a team and it's better to iron out all the wrinkles now and in private rather than waste your interviewees' time.

Exteriors

- Set up an exterior shot first of all. Check out your batteries...are they fully charged? Have you a spare set?

- Put the camera on the tripod. Is it level, are the settings on the pan and tilt head secure but offering you smooth movement if you need it?

- Is the cassette loaded? Is it numbered? Is the cassette box numbered?

- Is your clapperboard ready saying Test Shoot, Cassette 1, Shot 1?

- Is the microphone plugged in? Have you checked that the level is satisfactory through the headphones?

- Have you done a white balance?

Note: White balance is a method of setting the exposure for a video camera and most cameras use this method. Obviously the camera instruction book will give you precise details for the type of camera you are using but the principle is more or less the same on all cameras.

Some cameras have what looks like a white lens cap that fits over the lens, other cameras require you use a white sheet of paper and point the camera at it so that the camera can set its exposure level.

The whole idea is that you are giving the camera a preview of the level of ambient light so that it knows what settings to use.

If the light level changes, or the lighting situation changes in any way (for instance, if you are using artificial lights), always do a white balance.

Now select a shot and check out the framing. Look at the centre, then all round the edges of the shot. Check the space at top and bottom of frame and the space to the left and right. If a person is in the shot is there *looking room* at the side of the shot where that person is looking. If the person is walking is there *walking room* at the side of the shot towards which the person is walking?

Try some close-ups so that you become used to focussing sharply, for instance on a cutaway such as a buttonhole, spark-plug, watch. Practice, as always, makes perfect.

Shoot a slow pan, then take a wide shot of the same scene followed by closer shots. You'll be interested to see the results when you play it back!

Make sure you identify each shot with the clapper-board, and also 'log' each shot on your Shot List.

Interiors

Now move indoors and set up your camera again, this time to shoot an interview.

- First of all decide where your 'stand-in' interviewee is going to sit and look at the framing of the shot.

- Then set up for sound. Will you just be using the camera's built-in directional microphone? If so, is there a clock with a loud tick in line of sight with the camera? If there is, this may dominate the interview.

- Are you going to use two microphones? Many cameras have a stereo socket which allows you to use two microphones, one recording on the left channel and the other on the right hand channel. This can be very useful, because it will give you control over the sound levels at the editing stage.

- Who is going to 'monitor' the sound through ear-phones? Will it be the camera operator or somebody else? And what facilities will that person have to control the levels of the sound, e.g. to 'boost' a quiet interviewee?

- Check the shot again for trailing cables!

- Will you need artificial lights? You will have made notes about this at the recce so you should be able accurately to simulate some of the situations you will be in when you do the actual shoot.

Always check out the availability of natural light for an interview, including interior interviews, as a person seated by a window and lit by daylight can be an attractive picture and the daylight will give you natural 'modelling' on the face and give you accurate skin tones.

Artificial light

If you have to use artificial light don't mix it with daylight — it confuses the camera and you'll get very strange colours. Whole volumes have been written about lighting with all kinds of technical jargon about 'keylights', 'backlights', 'fill', 'North lights', 'Brutes', 'Bashers', 'Pups' and 'Inkie Dinkies'.

For our purposes I'd say 'keep it simple' and use your lights as 'bounce' lights to increase the overall light level in the room. What we mean by 'bounce' lights is that you point your light or lights at the ceiling. This will increase the light level so that the camera can cope and will give you even, shadow-free lighting.

Try it! Experiment with the lights and watch the interviewee's face in the viewfinder.

Then when you reckon you've got it right make a note of where the lights were in relation to the camera, the interviewee, the ceiling and so on. That way you'll be able to set-up quickly and efficiently on the day.

A quick aside about 'gels'. These are transparent pieces of perspex-like film that can be mounted over a lamp to change the colour of the light. A blue-ish gel can be used to simulate daylight for instance. Use with caution and take expert advice before you go down this path. And test it on camera...that's the point of this half-day practice shoot.

Before you record this 'lit' scene do a white balance again so that the camera knows what level of light it's getting and what kind of light. Check also with the camera instructions in case there is a filter you should use when shooting with artificial light. If in doubt don't 'mix' your light sources, say — daylight from a window supplemented by bounced artificial light. Draw the curtains instead!

When everything's ready shoot a sample interview from the top: clapperboard in, cue to start the interview, 'cut' to end a shot or end the interview. Check your shot list, see if the interview 'threw up' some cutaways that you might need. Discuss what these cutaways might be, and shoot them, shot list them, and discuss how they would be edited into the interview.

Play back the interview and discuss how it went:

- Was the shot all right or could it have been improved?

- What about the sound? Did clothes rustling (such as a silk blouse) spoil the sound track.

- What about the lighting?

- Was there too much, maybe making it all look a bit stark and clinical?

- Check everything out as if it were the real thing.

- If you hit a problem stop and sort it out straightaway.

If you have the time and the inclination shoot another interview with another 'dummy' interviewee. It'll give you useful experience in briefing people about the interview, putting them at their ease, placing microphones in the right place, moving lights around, changing camera positions, and doing it all quickly and without fuss.

Very soon you'll find that you are working as a team and more importantly you'll find that you are getting into a routine that more or less goes as follows:

Brief the interviewee. Set up the camera. Light the scene. White balance. Place the microphones. Sound test. Check the framing of the picture. Minutes of tape available? Cassette number, shot number, clapperboard, shot list. Notes taken during interview. Cutaways needed? Noddies or questions? Thank the interviewee. De-rig.

You will find that this practice session will have revealed weaknesses, which you can work on (such as unfamiliarity with bits of equipment and fitting all the bits together), and strengths which you can build on before the real filming begins. Most importantly the various roles you each play will have been acted out and how these roles relate to each other should by now be clear.

Practice Shoot — Summary

- Rig camera.

- Rig mics.

- White balance.

- Monitor sound.

- Use daylight if possible.

- Don't mix light sources.

- Discuss your test interview.

- Sort out problems as they occur.

- Do another test until you are happy.

Chapter Ten

THE SHOOT

It's Day One of your Shooting Schedule and the day before you will have double-checked the equipment list, made sure all the camera and lighting batteries are charged, and that you have blank cassettes ready for the shoot.

Your clapperboard should read 1/1/1 for Cassette 1, Shot 1, Take 1.

Arrive on time! If people are extending courtesies to you by letting you film on their premises or allowing you to interview them, then you can repay these courtesies by arriving and leaving on schedule.

You may recall that I stressed the importance of being honest with people, particularly concerning how long a filming session might take. Remember this and confirm it with your hosts when you arrive...it will re-assure them and it is part of your job to put them at their ease.

Before the interview starts, and before any filming starts remind them of what the video is about, what their part in it will be.

Repeat the assurance that you gave them earlier that they will have control over their input.

Then clearly and slowly explain to them what you plan to do in the next hour or so. "We want to talk to you about the time the factory closed. And then we'd be grateful if you would let us take some pictures of your press cuttings and your photograph album."

As you set up the equipment explain to your hosts what is happening.

"We're putting the camera over here because there's plenty of light coming in through the window, and we could sit together at this table and have our chat".

"Can we fasten this microphone to your lapel? Once we've done that we can forget about it and discuss what we're going to chat about".

"We're holding this card (clapperboard) up to the camera so we can keep track of what we're shooting! Just like the movies!"

"Mr Smith, what happened when they closed the factory?"

You're making a video and Mr Smith isn't even aware of the fact that you've started shooting! You just drifted gently into it.

Now the important thing is to retain control of that interview so that the information reaches you in fluent paragraphs rather than fragmented sentences.

So be prepared to go back and repeat a question in a different way, digress deliberately for a little while to instil confidence then return to the primary theme.

Above all *listen*! And always be patient, even when things seem not to be going as you planned.

The notetaker will be keeping a record of the shots as well as making notes about the interview, not only as a check against what cutaways you might need, but also as a brief record of what ground was covered in the interview.

Be prepared to stop and pause for breath. Take 2 might be that much fresher. And now you are working as a team you can all help the interviewer.

"I found it very interesting when Mr Smith talked about all those hundreds of men coming to work and finding the factory gates locked".

Encouragement, not criticism. So see if Mr Smith can enlarge on that scene, tell us what it felt like to be there, what his thoughts were at the time.

Cassette 1, Shot 1, Take 2!

When you've completed the interview double-check with the notetaker to make sure that you have covered the ground that you intended to cover.

Involve the interviewee in all of this. Tell him what you have learned from the interview and how you see this fitting in with other interviews you have planned. He may surprise you! After this informal 'de-briefing' many interviewees find that it triggers a host of memories or comments or other information.

So be prepared to shoot again, perhaps on another day when Mr Smith has had time to collect his thoughts...or perhaps then and there while it's fresh in his mind. This is the point where patience and sensitivity for your subject really come into play.

Remember that your own historical research could re-awaken his memories...names long forgotten, events dimly remembered could all come pouring back.

Now move on to the cutaways...and you should be ready with a list (!) not making them up as you go along.

So it's Mr Smith winding his watch, or lighting his pipe, or looking at the photographs on the mantlepiece, or whatever you have planned. And when you shoot those cutaways, including shots of family photographs, record for *at least* thirty seconds! So often people record a cutaway and count "One, Two, Three, There We Are! Cut!" and it is rarely long enough for your needs.

So shoot for at least thirty seconds, and don't feel silly if you record for a full minute. It's there if you need it.

Make sure you carefully list and identify each cutaway. If you are not going to do the final edit for some weeks after the shoot it is all to easy to forget whether Mr Smith aged fourteen was the boy on the left or the boy on the right.

Wallpaper

No, I'm not suddenly digressing into a home decorating course! 'Wallpaper' is industry jargon for fairly relevant shots that can be used to break up a long interview or even be used as a complete 'sequence' in your video. If you like 'wallpaper' is a sequence of cutaways but the shots are not normally as precise as 'Here I am on my Wedding Day' (cutaway wedding photo), but more "I get up at five every morning and walk through the fields to see the cattle". (Wallpaper shots coming down stairs, opening backdoor, putting wellies on, walking across fields, distant cattle seen through early morning mist).

So whilst you are shooting your cutaways just think about any wallpaper shots that you do while you are there that might be useful later, perhaps with a commentary laid over the shots. Sometimes a wallpaper shot can, surprisingly, 'make' a sequence.

Maybe you have Mr Smith coming into the room and sitting in his chair, lighting his pipe, and then taking out his scrap-book and having a browse.

The commentary might be "Mr Smith has lived all his life on the farm...a life full of memories."

If Mr Smith is not needed for these shots de-rig his microphone, thank him for the interview, and then explain what you are doing. Don't throw him on the garbage heap now you've wrung him dry! I've seen it happen. It really pays to think first about your subjects.

Tape recording and other sounds

A short digression that might be useful. You remember that I mentioned the possibility of taking a tape recorder with you during the original research visits. It can be more relaxing for the interviewee rather than have you sitting there scribbling notes. It can also help the interviewee become accustomed to bits of gadgetry being around.

There's no reason why you should not have a small recorder with you on location at the actual shoot. The notetaker might well find it useful and it will save your time and battery energy if you listen to a playback of the interview through the recorder rather than through the camera recorder.

Check before you shoot to see if you could transfer the sounds on this tape recorder to your final edited video.

I mention this because the cassette recorder could be useful for capturing those additional sounds that add atmosphere to your video...the village clock chiming the hour, the church bells on a Sunday morning, the distant sounds of traffic or cattle.

You could use it to record a 'buzz track'. This is a track of continuous sound that is laid over a tape sequence that has been heavily edited and has therefore got a rather 'jumpy' soundtrack. Typical 'buzz-tracks' would be the interior of a room, farm-yard exterior, village street exterior.

Just tell everyone you are recording and ask them to keep very quiet and record two or three minutes of sound.

If it is technically impossible to transfer sound from your tape recorder to your final edit you can still use your video camera to record these buzz tracks. Just de-focus the camera so that when you come to editing you will know that these 'shots' are for sound-only use.

But make sure you list these 'shots' so that you find them later on at the editing stage.

Action sequences

We're not re-shooting *Gone with the Wind* but there will be occasions when you will be shooting an action sequence even if it is as simple as the local postman delivering the mail.

The mistakes most people make with this kind of sequence is to try and shoot the whole action in one shot, and this leads to ugly zooms, juddering pans, and awfully distracting shot composition.

Try and think it through beforehand. Imagine just what you want to see on the screen.

And think of it as a sequence:

Van approaches and stops. Postman gets out. Post-man walks to front porch. Postman knocks on door.

Exchanges words with farmer. Returns to van. Drives off.

If you tried to shoot this as one continuous shot you'd be all over the place. You'd be zooming out to make space for the postman as he gets out of the van, you'd be panning him to the front door and finding his nose is on the edge of the frame because your pan is too slow. The shot would be a mess, and what's worse you would find that because there is so much lens and camera movement it is almost impossible to edit it together to make a reasonable sequence.

However if you go:

Shot 1: Van approaches and stops...wide shot.

Shot 2: Tighter shot. Postman gets out of van and leaves shot.

Shot 3: Tight-ish shot showing front doorway. Postman enters, chats and leaves shot.

Shot 4: Back on the van including driver's door. Postman enters shot and gets into van.

Shot 5: Van drives off (wide shot).

These shots will edit easily together and will truncate the action in a professional way. By 'truncate' I mean shorten the time the action takes when edited as opposed to the time the event took in 'real' time.

Demonstrating skills

This is a different kind of action sequence and one that should have a real time context in your video.

71

So in this kind of sequence we wish to capture the reality, not truncate a familiar and predictable action.

You may therefore consider 'overlapping the action' (another industry jargon phrase) so that the skills being demonstrated are shown in toto in a wide shot, in close-up to show the details, and in real time...if it's a painstaking task show that it is painstaking.

By overlapping the action we mean getting the subject to do the same task at least twice.

Say the sequence is milking a cow.

Shot one would be a wide shot so that you see the farmer, the cow and the environment (cowshed) perhaps wide enough to show another cow being milked alongside.

Then change your camera angle and your shot size to show the farmer's hands milking the cow, and the milk going into the bucket.

In this case the farmer is not repeating his actions for you...you are lucky in that the task is repetitive.

But if it were a mechanic changing a sparking plug you would have to ask him to repeat the action once or twice so that you have the close-ups you need.

Then at the editing stage you can 'overlap' the action, and cut from wide shot to close-up and so on.

A brief word about changing the camera position and the angle when you change shots. A slight change always looks better than just a change from wide to narrow angle on the zoom. When you cut the 'lazy' shots together the picture leaps forward and can be disconcerting.

Only a slight change is needed and always keep shooting in the same general direction. Don't move the camera to the other side of the car or cow for instance. If you do the farmer or the mechanic will be facing in the wrong direction and the cut will look very odd.

Shooting in the same general direction means your pictures will edit smoothly together because there is 'continuity of direction'. Continuity is a specialist area in the film and television industry and experts are employed to make sure that the Roman soldiers don't wear wristwatches, or that John Wayne's gun doesn't appear on his left hip in one shot and his right hip in the next.

In a documentary we only need worry about continuity of time and continuity of direction...and they're both very easy to understand.

Continuity of time means that: if you spend two days shooting with somebody but want to imply that your scenes happened in one day, just make sure that your 'stars' wear the same clothes. So, if you spend two days filming the farmer milking his cows, knowing that the final edited scene will be as simple as "The farmer milks his cows twice a day" just make sure he wears the same clothes.

Continuity of direction means that if you see someone walking from left to right across the scene in Shot 1, your brain expects him to continue to walk from left to right in Shot 2. The thing to remember is "Was he/it going left to right?" Then in the next shot he/it must also be moving from left to right. It even applies to static objects such as a parked car. If the car is 'facing' left to right in Shot 1, it will look very odd if it is facing the other way in Shot 2.

If you imagine a line drawn through the middle of the car from rear to front, any shots from one side of that line will cut together. Cut in a shot filmed from the other side of the line and the car will be facing the wrong way, because you have 'crossed the line' or what is also called the 'optical barrier'.

Finally, as with cutaways, always shoot for a little longer than you think you need to. When the farmer stops milking don't stop the camera straight-away...the perfect edit could be as he leaves shot, or pats the cow by way of a Thank You!

The Shoot — Summary

- Check all equipment.

- Batteries charged.

- Explain what you are doing.

- LISTEN!

- De-brief the interviewee.

- Be prepared for Take 2 or a return visit.

- Check your cutaways.

- Think about 'wallpaper'.

- Remember relevant sounds.

- Do you need a buzz track?

- Plan the action sequences.

- Plan how you can compress or truncate the action.

- Overlap the action in a demonstration.

Chapter Eleven

EDITING

Editing can be as simple or as complex as you wish to make it. As you developed your outline shape, your Draft Script and your various Shooting Schedules you will have become aware of the degree of complexity you are likely to undertake when editing.

But before you edit anything go back to the basic question "Who Is this video for?". We are not setting out to emulate a sophisticated broadcast documentary. We are making a watchable record for a contemporary audience (an audience that we know personally such as friends, relatives, colleagues, neighbours) and maybe for a future audience as yet unborn.

If you are making a video that is partly historical (our village, our factory, our family) keep the future audience in your mind throughout the shooting and editing stage. For instance, you may feel it unnecessary to show a map of your county, or to say in your commentary that the village is in Videoshire. But Videoshire may cease to exist in future years and the map might help a future generation identify the new name of the county.

Don't try and emulate what you see on television too closely because the television programme maker has to appeal to a totally different audience and edits his documentary with enough 'pace' to stave off 'channel hopping' by the viewer.

So a three-minute talking head might prove too slow and potentially boring to a producer hoping to retain the interest of millions of initially uninterested viewers.

You, on the other hand, must consider that this same three-minute talking head is what it is all about...The Man Who Was There Talking About It. Grandpa's memories of World War 2: his words, his face, no clever cutting. The truth.

Who your audience is and the aims of your project will dictate the style and pace of your edited video, and your editing will be governed by these parameters.

You may decide that future historians will be best served by a 'stark' style of editing such as a commentary naming the farmer, a map showing where his farm is, and then basically unedited interviews with the farmer, ending perhaps with a slow paced demonstration of the hand milking process.

On the other hand you may decide that a contemporary audience will be best served by a more sophisticated style of editing with lots of shots of the village and of people they know, with the interviews cut into smaller sequences devoted to the farmhouse, the farm, the herd, machine milking, hand milking, contemporary farm economics, how the farm and the farmer fit into village life and the village economy.

These ideas should have been given serious consideration at the planning stage and the style of editing should be easily forecast by looking at your Draft Script.

But your ideas may have changed whilst making the video, your conception of the potential audience may also have altered, and you might also have discovered, whilst shooting the video, that a simpler approach might be more effective.

But this is the stage when you really must make firm decisions. You have your raw material, the 'rushes'. Now you must decide how you will use that raw material. Take some time to think things through yet again.

Viewing rushes

Sit down and view your tapes (your rushes or raw material). Double check your shot lists against the notes you are now making, just in case there are two Shot 1/1/1, or two cassettes have the same number. Even the best notetakers make mistakes, or a clapperboard is not very clear, or a label slides off a cassette. So now is the time to get that side of things sorted and in order. Proper preparation can save frustration at a later stage.

As you view the tapes make copious notes about them so you really can remember clearly what they contain. 'Farmer milking' is not good enough. "Close up farmer's hands milking with bucket bottom of frame and milk squirting into bucket" is better, and it's better still if there's an extra note such as 'Farmer's wife seems to milk more slowly but has a steadier rhythm and fills the bucket more quickly!'

That kind of additional note might reap dividends later on when you remember that the farmer's wife in an interview actually makes the claim that women are better milkers than men!

Identify the best shots and the best material, and again make sure your notes make sense to everyone.

For instance:

3/12/1. Interview farmer's wife. About meeting farmer, and wedding day. Not very good...stilted.

3/12/2. Interview farmer's wife about meeting farmer at a village dance (he was so clumsy) and about wedding day (they had to go from the church to milk the cows and then go back to the reception to cut the cake).

Now we know that 3/12/1 is unlikely to be used and we know that 3/12/2 is fun and might be useful when we want some light relief. Or the farmer's version of how they met might be quite different and very effective and revealing when juxtaposed with his wife's version of events.

Find a way of making these good shots and sections leap out of the page at you, perhaps a big asterisk, or a coloured marker.

And don't forget to listen to the sound as well and make appropriate notes (Church bells over this? Wedding photos?).

Assembly order

Now that you have listed all your shots and know where everything can be found you can begin to think about a rough Assembly Order.

Your Draft Script may help here. In fact if everything went exactly to plan you may find that creating an Assembly Order is just a question of writing in the shot numbers to replace your original numbers.

So Shot 1 of your Draft Script becomes 3/14/1 for instance.

Even if you have modified things as the shooting went along you should still find that it echoes the original structure to some extent, and therefore your Editing Script or Assembly Order will basically be a re-write of your original Draft Script.

The major difference will be that you should allow more space for notes about sound (church bells over this shot), and also in the sound column allow space for the text of your commentary, even if it is only still in rough stage.

If you don't envisage a total re-write of your Draft Script you could photocopy it and then cut and paste it on to several sheets of paper to give yourself the extra space.

Sequence **B** on the Draft Script looked like this you may recall:

B   3   LS Village   VO   Ext.
Intro to Village
               4 High Street

     5   Church

     6   Domesday Book Mary

     7   Map   Mary

And here's what it could look like after a 'cut and paste'.

Editing script

B   2/12/3 LS Village   VO: This is West Ditton
                                in Northamptonshire

     2/15/1 High Street   A village in the
                                heart of England

     2/17/1 Church   St Mary Church is
                                one of the finest
                                examples of Saxon
                                architecture in
                                Britain

4/28/1 Domesday Book   Called West Ditch in
                        the Domesday Book
                        it had a population of
                        140 souls plus some
                        200 in neighbouring
                        hamlets.

4/33/1 Map   Close by are Rugby,
                        Northampton and
                        Daventry.

Cut and paste your Draft Script in this way (or use a word processor if you have access to one) and you will soon have a detailed Assembly Script.

Leave plenty of space for additional notes, such as music you may want to use, or additional sounds.

Write your draft commentary as you go along as this will give you an idea of how the video is 'flowing', and you can check it and modify it before you start the actual editing. You begin in this way to start thinking of pictures and words together.

For instance, the map in sequence **B** might show the M1 motorway and you may want to add a line of commentary to point this out. Or you may remember that your 'rushes' include a signpost at the village crossroads pointing to the towns and indicating how many miles to each town you have mentioned...so you may wish to add that shot.

When you have completed your commentary time each section, shot by shot, then check against your 'rushes' list to make sure that the shots you have will be long enough. You can then think of additional shots that you might use or alternatively shorten that bit of commentary.

Notice that we are planning everything on paper first of all, and in great detail. It may appear slow and laborious but believe me it will pay off when you start editing.

Editing — equipment

As with the camera equipment it is not my intention to go into great technical detail because of the wide range of equipment available and the even greater variety of knobs and dials and buttons. The principles though, whatever the sophistication (or otherwise) of your equipment are the same.

Basically we are talking about copying picture and sound from our original video cassettes and sound cassettes on to another tape so we need two machines — a playback machine with the original material and a record machine which will be used to 'build' our final video.

However, you may well find when you look at your instruction manuals that you can use the camcorder as the playback machine and there will be instructions on how to do this.

Set up your two machines. I always like to have the playback machine on the left as I face it and the record machine on the right, and check out the connecting cables and plugs and sockets.

Next see what sound/audio capabilities you have, such as a microphone socket, a socket for an external tape recorder or audio cassette player, and check out what kind of cable and plug connectors you might need.

Then look at the sound track facilities that are available to you. For instance, it may be possible for you to copy across your basic material on to audio Track 1 on your record machine, and then put commentary, music, etc on to Track 2.

Then check out what control you have over the sound level of each track. It may be a knob that you can rotate to a given setting or it may be a fader/lever that you can raise or lower to control the volume.

Now with the help of your various instruction manuals check out how a vision, or a sound and vision edit happens. Some systems require you to 'mark' only the 'In' point, that is the point at which the new picture gets added on to your assembly. Other systems like you to mark the 'In' and the 'Out' point as well so that you are copying across a precisely timed shot. The most sophisticated systems use time coding to give 'frame perfect' edits — study the manuals!!

When you've done all this *don't* start editing!

Check it all out again, read the instructions again.

Practice edit

Don't plunge into editing.

First of all write down a list of 'How To's' that every-one understands and check each stage as you go along.

This could be a summary of your various instruction manuals, but by writing down a summary you are becoming more familiar with the various oper-ational procedures and the names of the knobs and buttons and faders.

Also you will save yourself hours of time later on thumbing through the manuals to find the relevant instruction.

So this summary could include things like:

- How to record a commentary.

- Plug microphone into right hand audio socket, Track 2, far right of machine. Set Track 2 volume level to 5. Set Track 1 volume level to 0.

- Mark 'In' point of sound edit.

- Make sure you are only sound editing, not picture editing.

- Perform edit and at edit point speak.

- Rewind tape and set Track 1 Volume to 5.

- Replay tape to check edit and volumes.

When you're happy with this summary sheet check the various knobs and dials so that you know where they are and what they do, and if you think it might help you, consider sticking coloured tape over some of them to help you find them easily. Maybe some red tape over a vision or audio record button, as an additional warning that you might wipe or overwrite something.

Now do some practice editing.

Copy some material across and then play it back to see that you have joined the two machines together correctly. Check out what happens to the sound.

Does Track 1 sound on the playback machine emerge safely on Track 1 sound of the record machine or have you got your wires (literally) crossed? More coloured tape?

Once you are happy that sound and pictures are being copied from the playback machine to the record machine, try a basic sound and picture edit.

Check what the record machine has received. Was it *exactly* the material you wanted it to receive?

Look again at the kind of control your machines can offer you, such as only sending Sound Track 1, or letting you send a mix of Sound Track 1 and Sound Track 2 to Sound Track 1 on the record machine.

- Can the machines do this? Can you do it?

- Can you control the mix of sound levels reaching Track 1 of your record machine?

Try it once or twice until you are in charge of things. If you have problems go back to the beginning.

Now send only Track 1 sound and add some commentary to Track 2 of your record machine.

- Play it back. Is it OK? If not why not?

- Is the commentary too loud? If so, adjust and repeat until you find the right level...and then modify your Instructions Summary accordingly.

As you learn how to do things always add to or modify your Instruction Summary so, if you return to your editing after a holiday or a long time away on business the notes are there to refresh your memory.

Now try editing in a cutaway to the material you have on your record machine. Remember we are now talking about a picture-only edit.

Try it. Play it back:

- Is the sound untouched (the way you want it)?

- Did the cutaway arrive exactly when you wanted it to and then disappear exactly when you wanted it to?

Perhaps you are not being as accurate as you should be selecting your 'Ins' and 'Outs'.

Or maybe the machinery is not very accurate and 'drifts' by up to a second. (This can happen). If this is the case do several edits to try and find where the 'drift' is, that is to say is it at the 'In' point or the 'Out' point? Identify it and make a note in your Instructions Summary.

First assembly

Once you are completely familiar with your equipment and have confidence in your ability to edit, add commentary and drop in cutaways, you are ready to begin the First Assembly, rather like laying down the keel and ribs of a ship.

By First Assembly I mean joining the main ingredients together following your Editing Script sequence by sequence. The Second or Final Assembly is when you add your commentary and replace parts of an interview with cutaways (though keeping the interview sound running).

In the sequence that we 'cut and pasted' you could either edit the shots together (though timed to fit your proposed commentary), or you could lay the commentary first and then add the shots to fit.

If you have a music sequence you would lay the music down first and then edit the pictures to fit.

Once those vital elements are in place the rest will slot in with ease and surprising rapidity. So:

- You have viewed your raw material and logged every shot.

- You have made a note of the 'gems'.

- You know where to find every shot.

- You have a detailed Assembly Script.

- You are familiar with the editing techniques.

So you really can begin, and all I would remind you of, as I did with the original Shooting Script, is to work in sequences and, before you start to edit, think the sequence through as carefully as you can.

Your final video may consist of hundreds, even thousands of shots...a daunting thought. But it may be six or fifteen sequences...a figure we can cope with. So edit your video sequence by sequence. You'll be aware of the progress you are making as you complete each sequence, you'll be able to concentrate on the detail within the sequence without the distraction of thinking "three thousand more shots to go", and editing sequence by sequence allows you to feel the shape and rhythm of your video as you work.

Titles may be something you would put off until you have finished the video and that's fine. But if you decide to do that remember to leave space at the front of the video otherwise you'll have shot yourself in the foot!

So before you start a sequence think it through. Is it going to be simply Shot 22 followed by Shot 24 followed by Shot 18. Or is it going to be Shot 22 with a commentary on Track 2, then Shot 24 (the interview) with cutaways from the family album that you will add at Final Assembly, then Shot 18 with sound of distant bells because your next shot, and the starting shot of the next sequence, is to be the village church?

Decisions! Decisions! — but make them before you edit.

- Maybe you do your commentary as you go ... that's fine.

- Maybe you pre-record your commentary and edit it in as you go...that's fine too if you've timed your shots correctly or have sufficiently long shots to cover slight timing discrepancies.

- Maybe you record your commentary when all the picture editing is complete...that's my favourite way because the commentary flows naturally, but you must have done your commentary and shot timing homework in the first place.

'... called West Ditch in the Domesday Book ...'

All three methods can work perfectly well but I hope you can understand the need to make decisions of this kind before the editing starts, that you understand the need for accurate timing, and that you have thought through carefully which track will have what, where you might want to 'stretch' a cutaway so that the viewer can have a good long look at the wedding photo, and how you will begin and end each sequence.

A technical aside: your videotape has basically four 'tracks' — picture, sound 1, sound 2, control track.

The control track is like the sprocket holes in a movie film...it keeps everything flickering along at the same speed and thus keeping the picture steady.

Check out the options available to you as you can 'assemble' edit or 'insert' edit. With assemble edit you build up your video bit by bit but the control track is also added bit by bit so you can get a 'jerk' at each edit. With 'insert' editing you lay a continuous control track on your 'record' tape before you start editing and thus get better joins. So it's worth checking out.

Commentaries and cutaways

We've touched on 'stretching' a cutaway so that the viewer can have a longer linger over the wedding photograph, but it's a serious point and will have a direct bearing on your commentary. So rehearse any edits involving commentary and cutaways to help you decide how long that 'linger' should be. You can always 'pause' the commentary as we see the bride's dress for the first time to allow for all the "Aaaaghs" of the doting aunties watching your video. At the end of the day, the pace of the film — whatever you include and what you exclude — is your decision. Think!

Several books could be written about commentary writing and it is not my intention to write yet another volume. All I will say is that it is there to give additional information and to enhance the viewer's understanding of your video.

And an essential part of a good commentary are the silences, where the picture tells its own story without distractions. Feel free to run several seconds of that wedding photograph in total silence, give your viewer 'thinking' time, time to digest what has been said on commentary or in interview.

As to additional information, I mean relevant additional information, so often we hear commentaries that tell us what we already know:

> *Shot*: Betty in a Blue Car.
> *Commentary*: "Betty has a blue car".

Or the commentary conflicts (and therefore distracts):

> *Shot*: Betty in a Blue Car.
> *Commentary*: "The Stock Exchange crash of 1992 had no effect on West Ditton."

Better would be:

> *Shot*: Betty in a Blue Car.
> *Commentary*: "Betty is the local doctor and visits old people in the outlying hamlets every Monday".

Use commentary to provide that additional information that you know to be factually correct and of interest. When in doubt settle for silence!

If you've followed me so far your Final Assembly should be no more than an extra cutaway here, and a word of commentary there...and it's done!

Editing — Summary.

- Bear future audience in mind.

- View and list your rushes.

- Make an Assembly Order or Editing Script.

- Know your equipment.

- Practise editing.

- Work in sequences.

- Commentaries complement the pictures.

- Silence is golden.

- Allow linger time over cutaways.

Chapter Twelve

THE PREMIERE AND BEYOND

You've added your titles, those extra cutaways, and your commentary flows along. So you're ready for your first showing and it has to be the farmer and his wife...after all they are the stars. (Or the bride and groom, or the staff instructor).

I'd suggest that they have a private viewing rather than put them in the front row of the village hall. Seeing themselves on screen might be a shock, even if you've involved them at the editing stage to check out some facts. The completed video with titles, music and commentary is something quite different and they should be given the chance to adjust.

Later you can throw the days open to the history society, or the entire family, or school or the village and no doubt you will glow with pride for some time...and rightly so.

But then what?

People may ask for copies. Remember to give the farmer one!

And your video may have some archival value. If it's about a new technique at work other branches of your company might benefit from a copy. Or your company might want to keep footage of the *old* ways of doing things. If your video is about your community, such as a factory closing down or an orchard being replaced by a supermarket your local library might like a copy, or the county archivist, the head teacher, the local newspaper.

Plus specialist national historical archives, such as the British Video History Trust who might show your video to a television producer twenty years from now!

Imagine it....your video making television history.

> *Shot*: Betty in a Blue Car!
> *Commentary*: In the Twentieth Century people travelled in metal containers called cars.

Good shooting!

Further reading:

Shooting on Location by Peter Jarvis

Editing Film and Videotape by Ed Boyce, et al

From Script to Screen by Gordon Croton

Stand By Studio! by Brian Phillips

After Tea We'll do the Fight: Filming Action by Mike Crisp

Continuity Notes by Roger Singleton-Turner

Narration and Editing by John Mansfield

Music and Sound Effects by John Mansfield

The Production Assistant's Survival Guide by Cathie Fraser

The Television Researcher's Guide by Kathy Chater

Teletalk: A Dictionary of Broadcasting Terms